my first car

my first

car

by james lecesne
additional interviews by marion long

CROWN TRADE PAPERBACKS NEW YORK

The following interviews by Marion Long originally appeared in *GQ* magazine: Dan Aykroyd, Roy Blount Jr., Zbigniew Brzezinski, Art Buchwald, Johnny Carson, John Glenn, Hugh Hefner, Lee Iacocca, Jeremy Irons, Al Jarreau, Stephen King, Liberace, John McEnroe, Ralph Nader, Dan Rather, Ronald Reagan, Andy Warhol, Tom Wolfe.

Art Director: Wynn Dan   Designer: Trey Speegle

Published by Crown Trade Paperbacks, 201 East 50th Street, New York, New York 10022. Member of the Crown Publishing Group. Random House, Inc. New York, Toronto, London, Sydney, Auckland

Crown Trade Paperbacks and colophon are trademarks of Crown Publishers, Inc.

Manufactured in Singapore

Library of Congress Cataloging in Publication Data
Lecesne, James
My first car / by James Lecesne
          p.   cm.
1. Automobiles—United States.   2. Celebrities—United States—Biography.
I. Title.
TL23.L367   1993
629.222—dc20   92-24109 CIP

ISBN 0-517-88000-8

10 9 8 7 6 5 4 3 2 1

First Edition

"*GQ* published its *My First Car* feature in July 1984, and it remains one of the most popular articles we ever ran. First cars, like first loves, are indelible, eternal in the minds of men and women."

—Art Cooper
Editor-in-Chief, *GQ*

Half of the royalties from the sale of this book will go to: M.A.D.D. MOTHERS AGAINST DRUNK DRIVING

contents

© Anthony Russo

My father, to whom this book is dedicated, was mad about cars. From the time he arrived in this country from the West Indies at the age of seventeen until his death last year, the automobile business was his passion and his livelihood. He began as a stock boy for a Ford dealership in the Bronx and eventually became the top dealer of Ford parts in the United States, a position he held for many years, topping himself, winning awards and trips around the world. He took special pride in his ability to recite the catalog and call number of any part, large or small, belonging to any Ford since 1940. If pressed, he could do the same with Chevrolets and Buicks. Fords, however, were his forte.

At least once a year, my father would thrill us kids by pulling up to our suburban home in a brand-new family car (a Ford), each one smarter, shinier and more innovative than its predecessor. The day was unannounced but this event was always followed by an inaugural ride through the three neighboring towns and usually ended up at the local Dairy Queen or Howard Johnson. Cars were a big deal in my family—all twenty-seven of them.

I did not follow in my father's footsteps, however, so in 1972, when it came time for me to buy my own first car, I naturally turned to him with the $400 I made as a cashier at the Grand Union. He brought home a 1965 Rambler American and offered his apologies. It was the best he could do, he said, and it was not a Ford. Known among my friends as "the Black Death," as much for its dead-black finish and blood-red upholstery as it was for my dubious driving skill at the time, this car was mine, my first—without apology—and I loved it. Like any seventeen-year-old, I knew that the clearest road to freedom was the one that stretched out in front of my first car.

Whatever our individual first car experience may have been, it seems that we've all had one. Whether it was a hard-earned $100 heap of junk or a Happy Birthday hot rod with love from Mom and Dad, whether it represented a rite of passage from dependent adolescence to freewheeling adulthood, or simply another adult convenience, that first car remains for many, like the first fling at love, an unforgettable experience.

"I was living in Czechoslovakia, and it was probably in the year 1967. I was studying at the Charles University of Prague, and my parents were living in a town which is called Zlin. I was driving this car, it was a Fiat, a mini 600, it was navy blue and it was adorable. This was in the sixties of Flower Power and the Beatles, and I was a young girl. I got stickers of different flowers, like daisies, and I put them all over my car.

"Now, at that time, I had an apartment in Prague and every day on my way to school I came to a crossroad. I was never able to make a left turn on that crossroad. I was supposed to either go through a tunnel, which would take me another ten minutes around the town, or I had to go straight, which would take me another half hour to get to school. So, every day, I made this left turn. There was always a policeman standing on the road. There was also a station for the electric trollies. So what I would do was wait for a trolley with three or four cars to come by, and I would go around it. Of course, the policeman was in the center. While the trolley was making a left turn, I was making a left turn with it. He could never catch me.

"Finally, one day, I don't know what went wrong. After three or four years of making constant turns on this road, he got me. He said, 'You made this turn!' I panicked and started to cry, I told him I'm from a different town and I got lost. He said, 'You have been making this turn at this crossroad for the last five years!' And it was the daisies that gave me away!

"I was a devil with this car. I miss it."

IVANA TRUMP *is a mother and a businesswoman. For city driving she now prefers a 1991 560 SEL and a driver.*

ivana trump

"It had no brakes, it barely had a clutch, and to get it started you had to push it out into the street, run with it and then pop the clutch. It was a Volkswagen, given to me as a gift or I traded something for it, something strange. The color? It was a kind of third-day period red as I remember it. I learned to drive in this car, round and round in a parking lot, popping the clutch. It was really ridiculous. I had it about four or five years, until I finally traded it in for a moped.

"It was a great car, but I could never just go somewhere; I had to have somebody to look and make sure the traffic was stopped and stand behind the car to give that initial push so that I could run with it, jump it and pop it. Whenever I left the house, I had to leave with a friend or knock on someone's door and see if they were home.

"Once I learned to drive, I could actually get into my car and, with a little help, just go. I could get my kid, get in the car and we could go drive around the block just because we felt like it.

"The thing I remember most about that car is this one day I couldn't find my kid. She wrote me a little note saying that she had run away. I looked everywhere for her and I got really worried. As I was coming back home, I happened to pass the Volkswagen and there she was asleep in the backseat of the car. She had run away to the car."

WHOOPI GOLDBERG *is a comedian and an Academy Award–winning actress.*

"The first car I owned was a 1938 Ford Coupe with 60 horsepower. It was like a large Volkswagen Beetle. I remember it well. My father bought it for me in the summer of '42, after my first year in college.

"When I graduated with a master's in engineering from Princeton in 1946, I went right to work at Ford and got another car. My father had paid $275 for that first one, and I sold it five years later for $400. You should mention that cars were hard to come by, but I suppose I was a pretty good salesman even then."

LEE IACOCCA *is retired Chairman of the Chrysler Corporation.*

"My first car was a 1939 green Chrysler Royal. It was my father's car, so it was free. I got it when I was a junior at Norfolk High School in Nebraska.

"The most memorable experience I had in the car was losing my virginity. As in all small towns in those days, there were 'nice girls,' girls that you married—and girls that you did not. Well, in Norfolk, there was this girl, I'll call her Francine, and Francine, well, 'put out'—at least that was the story that was going around. When I finally got up enough nerve to ask her out and she said yes, you can imagine my excitement—Mount Vesuvius! However, I had one problem to overcome: protection. I went up to the drugstore counter, and the druggist hollers, 'Well, John, what can I do for you?' Luckily, he saw that I had Francine waiting in the car and knowingly handed over the goods. I remember I had, as we used to put it, a 'swell' time.

"I still have the car. A steelworker in Norfolk restored it beautifully and NBC gave it to me as a birthday present. The car doesn't have quite the pickup it used to, but then neither do I."

JOHNNY CARSON *hosted the* Tonight Show *for over thirty years. He now drives a white Corvette.*

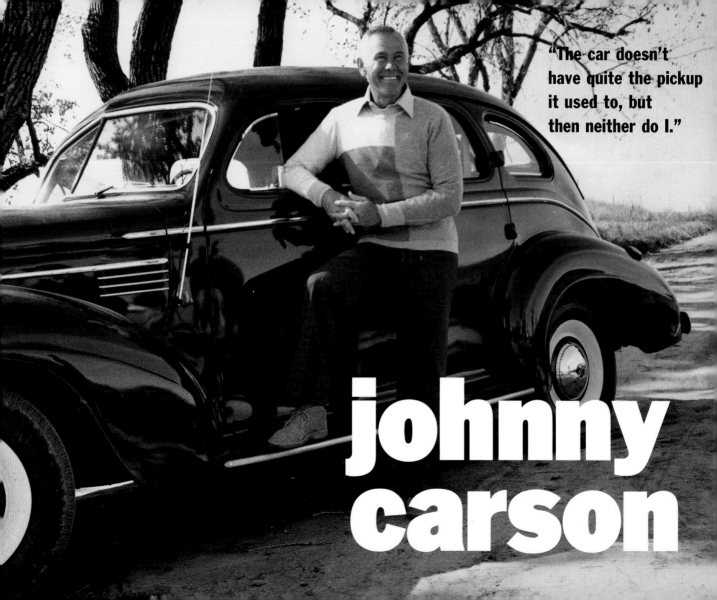

"The car doesn't have quite the pickup it used to, but then neither do I."

johnny carson

"It was the 'hot tip' of the moment, a very popular car in those days, a '57 Chevy, red and white, red with a white top, two-door, hardtop Belair. I was born and raised in Italy, but I've lived in Nazareth since I was fifteen years of age. We used to have a lot of fun around here just dragging away. With that car we were the Kings of the Road. When I say 'we,' I mean my twin brother, Aldo, and I. We owned it together and we used to take turns driving it. After school, we used to work with an uncle of ours to earn a little bit of change. We staggered it: I worked one day, he worked the other, so it turned out to be a perfect arrangement for both of us.

"We didn't do much work on the car. We couldn't afford it, to be honest. But the car was incredible. It came out of

mario andretti

the box really great. There was another fellow, his nickname was Knaussie, and he owned a white '57 Chevy that was perhaps our biggest adversary. He spent so much money on his car—different shafts, dual carburetors and all that kind of thing—but he could never beat us. We had a stock 283 engine with a Dontov cam.

"Zora Dontov [the inventor of the Dontov cam] was a mythical figure to us; he was actually 'Mr. Corvette' for General Motors at that time, quite a venerable individual. It was strange that we eventually met him and struck up a very warm relationship. I've known him for many years.

"I've had many, many cars since, but that's probably the only car I was ever really in love with. For my fiftieth birthday, friends presented me with a huge cardboard of a '57 Chevy. Those times are behind now, but I will always remember them with fondness."

Three-time winner of the Indy 500, MARIO ANDRETTI *won his first race in his red '57 Belair.*

tommy tune

Drawing by Eric Palma originally in the New Yorker © 1989.

PALMA

"Mine is a very sad story. I still have dreams about it. I don't carry any regrets about life, but this is the closest I've come to having a regret. It was Christmas morning, and we were all in the living room. I opened a present. It was a key, and I just knew. I ran outside and there under the carport was a brand-new Model T. It was in spic-and-span condition, with a big red bow around it. It was shiny, shiny black, lacquered black with a thin, thin racing stripe all around its middle. And my heart just sank to the bottom of my bowels. I hated it. I hated it because, at that time, I went to a high school where everyone drove Thunderbirds. The thought of having to drive up to school in a

> "It was Christmas morning. I opened a present. It was a key, and I just knew."

Model T...I just didn't have the style and confidence to pull it off. My father was so proud of that car. I think it was the first car he'd ever seen. A Model T, a Model Tome they used to call it, and my name being Tom. I never drove it. It just sat there and sat there until it rusted. I remember my mother driving it once. She piled in a bunch of people, and I reluctantly got into the backseat. But I never sat in the driver's seat of that car. Never. Finally we put an ad in the paper, and someone came over and bought it. I don't think it even worked anymore. Isn't that a strange story? So unlike me. And it really broke Father's heart. But you know—kids."

TOMMY TUNE *is an award-winning director, choreographer and entertainer.*

"It was a '66 Mustang owned by the proverbial little old lady in Bel Air, who had only driven it to church."

"I lived in New York City for ten years, and who needs a car in New York? But L.A. is such a car culture. I couldn't be seen in just anything; the choice was very important since here it's a reflection on one's character. I must say that my boyfriend took the bull by the horns and decided that I should have something cool to drive around in. He found it in the *Recycler*, which is a newspaper for used goods. It was a '66 Mustang owned by the proverbial little old lady in Bel Air, who had only driven it to church. I bought it in 1987 and it only had 57,000 miles on it. The day we got it, it broke down on the highway. We took it to a lot of mechanics and none of them could tell us what the hell was wrong with it. But then the Miracle Armenian Mechanic fixed it and there hasn't been a major problem with it since.

"I've put tons of money into it, rebuilt the engine and had two paint jobs trying to duplicate that great color—it was blue with an aqua hue, so sixties, and really couldn't be duplicated. It didn't have air conditioning,

ann magnuson

but there were only a couple of months of the year when this was a problem and even then I didn't mind. I have a habit of putting myself through discomfort for long periods of time. I'm not sure why. Maybe it's penance for having lived a cushy suburban childhood.

"I still have the Mustang. I can't bring myself to sell it; I'm a huge sentimentalist. I mean, I have platform shoes from the seventies that I would never part with because they remind me of a few incredible evenings. When I think of my first car, I remember where I lived at the time, of how I had just moved in with my boyfriend. That car resonates with a lot of love.

"Even though I drive a more environmentally correct Volvo now, I'm holding on to the Mustang as a collector's item and keeping it for those special occasions. I'll wait till the wolves are at the door before I sell that car."
ANN MAGNUSON, *actress, comedian and writer, lives and drives in Los Angeles.*

"The year is 1948. I am twenty-seven years old and a very successful portrait, theatrical and dance photographer working for the *New York Times* European edition in Budapest. A car was an utmost luxury in postwar Europe, especially in the Russian satellite country of Hungary, where I was living. But private enterprise was still allowed and so I could buy a car. It was a used Opel Kadett, four-cylinder, shift car, and the body was a mess. But at the time, I did not know how a car could look, so for me it was a wonderful vehicle with four wheels, low on gas, nice, sporty, red and mine. I named the car 'My Baby.'

"I had already put 40,000 kilometers into that car and lots of repair money to keep it going, when a curious order came down from our communist government...one of their numerous orders called 'salami tactics' because every day a slice of our freedom was sliced away. Every day a new law was voted on by a rubber-stamp parliament and enforced the next day. So the order came out on December 27th of 1951 that by the 30th of December all private cars had to be turned in for government use. Some wise patriot had decided that private cars consumed too much gas, they were a luxury and we now cannot afford luxury! Last names from A to K had to deliver their

bela kalman

"I came to Vienna on foot in 1956. I've had a car ever since."

cars to a garage on the beautiful Margarete Island in the middle of the Danube in downtown Budapest; the others, somewhere else. My Baby went to the island. The government announcement said that the 'former owners' would be compensated—another commie lie as it turned out. So my car went down to the underground garage on the island of Margarete, and I came up and home on foot.

"I came to Vienna on foot in 1956. I've had a car ever since."

BELA KALMAN *is a distinguished photojournalist. In 1991, Bela won a red Mercedes convertible at a raffle; she gave it to her husband for his seventieth birthday.*

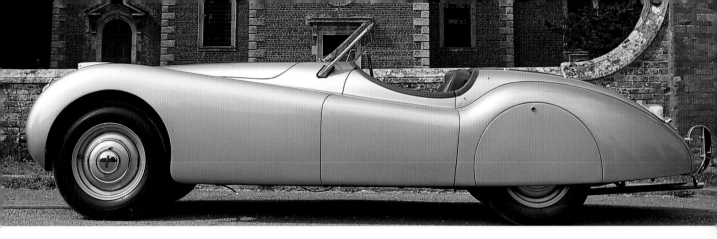

"I've only had two cars in my life, and I got the first car not because I wanted to drive, but because I thought it was so beautiful I wouldn't mind sitting in it and having it.

lena horne

"I was in England in 1950. I saw a picture of a Jaguar in a magazine, and I was driven down to Coventry, England, which was still recovering from the battering it had taken in the war. The factory had just begun to work again, and they invited me over. I was working there in the theater at the time. And I went to see the cars that they were starting to make. I ordered my car. It was a Mark IX, silver-gray Jaguar sedan with an English drive-side and lipstick-red upholstery. They made it for me, and after a few months they shipped it on a boat to America to me. It was the most beautiful car. We used to love riding in it down the avenues, because with the British-drive and my husband behind the wheel, it seemed like nobody was driving when they pulled up beside me. Everybody used to think it was a miniature Rolls-Royce; that's what everyone would ask when they pulled up beside us. We kept the car eighteen or twenty years because we loved it so. My memories of it were its great beauty and how wonderfully well it ran.

"By the way, I never learned to drive."

The legendary LENA HORNE *is a star of stage and screen. She currently resides in Manhattan without a car.*

"I didn't feel in a hurry to get a car or license. I lived away from home in high school, and the people I lived with had a son my age. He used to drive his parents' car and although I was double-dating just about all the time, I thought it was okay.

"My first car was a '78 TransAm. It was silver with a black interior. I paid $6,000 for it. About a month after I got my license I signed a professional contract. The first thing I did was go out and buy a car.

"I think the thing I remember most about the car was the reason I bought it, which was to use a CB radio. That was when the movie *Smokey and the Bandit* came out. I'll always remember that summer, driving around to Steak 'n Shake, and cruising around with a buddy of mine. He used the CB radio so much, I hardly got a chance to play with it. I was lucky because I bought it at the beginning of June and I was able to drive it June, July, August, September and October, and then I was sold—or traded—to Edmonton.

WAYNE GRETZKY, *known as "the Great One," plays hockey for the L.A. Kings.*

wayne gretzky

jeremy irons

"I left school at seventeen and before I started to study to be an actor, I worked as a social worker in South London. Free bed and board and £2.10 per week.

"One day hitchhiking to my parents' home for Sunday lunch, I was given a lift by a painter in a 1952 side-valve, rag-top Morris Minor. The car had leaf-green body work which had not seen wax for some considerable time. It smelt of Castrol R—a racing oil which it seemed to burn in profusion. Its top speed was 60 miles per hour and though till then I'd never had a car—I wanted it.

"I asked my driver to let me know if he could ever be persuaded to sell it. Two days later he called to say that if I cared to part with £5—the car was mine.

"I took a bus immediately with my older Scottish landlady to pick it up. On our drive home it immediately broke down outside the Houses of Parliament, but a push start with the landlady got it going again and we juddered home.

"Over the next months by various roadsides, I stripped down the engine and got to know it intimately while I taught myself rudimentary mechanics.

"I have rarely since felt the elation that Morris gave me as I drove her full of friends with the hood down.

"Now when a passing car gives me that evocative smell of Castrol R, I turn expectantly with the pleasure that certain perfumes still arouse in me.

"When she finally gave her last gasp, I towed her to a scrap yard in the country, where I was rewarded by my investment doubled—a ten-pound note!

"I would still rather have had her, though.

JEREMY IRONS *is an Academy Award–winning actor.*

"Are you asking the wrong guy—I hate driving! I'm a very bad driver. All my experiences have been lousy.

"The first vehicle I ever drove was when I was eighteen and in the Marine Corps. I was stationed on Eniwetok, an island in the Marshall Islands, and was with a fighter squadron as an ordnance man, which meant that I was involved with bombs and ammunition. The first time I drove anything, I was in the tent, and the gunnery sergeant said to 'take the bomb truck out to the line with the bombs on it.' I said, 'I've never driven before.' He said, 'Well, this is as good a time as any to start learning.' So the first vehicle I ever drove in my life was a bomb truck with about five hundred pounds of bombs on it. It was a drive of roughly a mile and a half. I lost about twelve pounds driving from the tent to the line. I think that could be the trauma that has followed me through the rest of my life.

"This experience was followed by a car that belonged to my college roommate at USC. I think it was a 1940 Ford with four doors. The brakes were no good. It was probably the most dangerous car on the road, and I was a very bad driver. If you saw a red light, you had to start pumping the brakes at least half a block away. I hated driving. I don't know why. Maybe it was because of the brakes.

"Then I went to Paris, and I didn't dare drive during my fourteen years there. I was scared of the French drivers. For my social evenings I took taxis. I guess it was okay with the women; nobody complained. They should only have realized how lucky they were.

"Then I came back to the U.S. in 1962, and for the first three or four years I'd ride with people. But because I wasn't driving I didn't have a license. And when you don't have a license, it's incredible, you can't do a thing. I couldn't cash a check. No one would trust me. One time I was in a store, talking with a saleswoman. She'd read every column I'd ever written. She even told me she was my biggest fan. Then when I tried to cash a check, she asked to see my driver's license. When I said I didn't have one, she wouldn't cash my check. She didn't trust me.

"So I got a license, and although I passed my driver's test, I never did learn parallel parking. Now I always park at the end of a street.

"I buy cars, but I don't drive them. I now have a 1974 Volvo that I keep on Martha's Vineyard, which has about 25,000 miles on it. And I have a 1980 Honda parked in front of my house, and that's got about 12,000 miles on it. So everybody says, 'Art, if you ever want to sell your car, let us know,' because I'm averaging less than the little old lady who only drives to church. I've never had a mishap, but I don't drive long enough: The odds are in my favor. If it's raining, I won't go out.

"I'm not like the other guys you've talked to. I don't want to hit the open road. I have no desire to own a Porsche. Cars don't turn me on. I started out with trauma, and I still have it. Every time I get into a car, I think I'm driving the bomb truck."

ART BUCHWALD *is a columnist and erstwhile humorist.*

barbie

Barbie, featured here in her first convertible, was unavailable for comment.

liliane montevecchi

"When I went to Hollywood I was nineteen. I had just left Paris after being prima ballerina with Roland Petit's ballet company, and I was under contract to MGM. I was there only one week, and I bought a Buick for fifty bucks. I remember it was yellow with two doors. You know, those old, old, old, old Buicks with only two gears and two doors? Such a funny-looking car, but I happened to like it, so I bought it on the spot.

"Every day I had to drive to the MGM studio and report to school. The first time I drove to the lot, the guards would not let me pass through the gates. Nobody was allowed in the MGM lot with such a car, they told me. But I suppose because it was me and I was so funny not being able to speak a word of English and with that funny-looking car, they let me in. This went on for a week. And I was so crazy with this car, this Buick. I drove all over the place with it. I don't remember ever getting rid of it, the thing just went to pieces, piece by piece until there was nothing! It was a lemon, as we say. I suppose that's why I bought it for only fifty bucks. After that I bought a Jaguar."

MISS MONTEVECCHI *is a Tony Award-winning Broadway performer and former star of the* Folies Bergere *in Paris.*

"It was a 1939 Dodge flathead six, four-door sedan with a three-speed shift on the column. It had a black paint job that was done with a broom, so that the marks, the brushstrokes, were quite evident on the sides; there were actual ridges of paint on the car. And that particular model had the suicide doors, you know, the back doors that opened out.

"My father bought it for for $125. I was the lucky fifth owner of the vehicle. My dad installed a cassette tape player in the dashboard and provided tapes by Benny Goodman, Jack Hilton, Freddy Gardner, Ray Noble—all the old 1940s swing bands. We'd drive in the car and play the old music, and it would really take us back.

"My friends and I went to college and went to concerts in it, and we dressed for the car—the double-breasted suit with the pleated pants, and the slicked-down hair. We tried to look as much as possible like soldiers from the Canadian army in 1939 having a civilian night out.

"In the wintertime when it snowed I used the old car to drag my friends behind me. They would put on heavy boots, hook on to the back bumper, and do what in Canada was called 'bunking.' I'd drag the boys behind the old Dodge—it was just like skiing, with a car pulling you. You just had to watch out for manhole covers.

"Somewhere, there's a beautiful shot of me and a friend sitting on the hood of this car. We look like two old crows sitting out in a field. Ken Danby, a Canadian Realist painter, has a painting called 'From the Summer of '38,' a beautiful picture, with what looks like my Dodge sitting in a field. That's exactly what happened to my first car: It ended up just like the one in that painting."

DAN AYKROYD *is one of the original Not Ready for Prime Time Players on* Saturday Night Live.

lily tomlin

"Somehow, we had hooked one of those little three-wheeled cars to our bumper and we just dragged it all the way to the First Street overpass where it finally flew free."

Risko

"I was born in Detroit, but we never had a car. It was unbelievable that you could live in the Motor City and never have a car. So when I was about seventeen and my brother was about thirteen, my father bought us a '58 Opal. It was the biggest thing in the world for us to have a car, and as soon as we got it we stayed out half the night.

"One night we were out at a party way over on the other side of town. We left the party real late, about 2 A.M. We start driving home and right away we realize there is a car following us; it's close to our bumper and they've got their lights out. We start trying to ditch them, but this old Opal can't do anything. No matter what we did, this car stayed right with us. We just could not shake it for anything. Finally when we were almost to our house, I said to my brother, 'Get ready to make a run for it.' So when we pulled up in front of our house, we threw open the car doors and ran up to the porch and into the house as fast as we could. When we looked out the window, the Opal was just sitting there with an Isetta hooked to its bumper. Somehow, we had hooked one of those little three-wheeled cars to our bumper and we had dragged it all the way from the East Side. That was the first car we ever had.

"The first car I ever owned by myself was a '69 Firebird. I bought it in '69 at the end of the year, because it was cheaper. The only color they had left was that awful army green. It was a convertible with one of those big engines. That was the year I joined 'Laugh In.' I had it driven all the way from New York to California, because I was so attached to it. I had it for years. It was really banged up. Everybody kept saying to me, 'Just get a new car!' But I thought if I run into a fence with a new car I'll be miserable. Years later people would razz me and say, 'Remember when you were first on "Laugh In" and you'd come onto the lot with that old green Firebird, and the front fenders were all banged up and dented? We used to call it "The Tank."'

"Eventually something went wrong with it. If you made a very sharp turn at a very slow speed, it would sheer off a nut or something and the front axle would drop off on one side or the other. This happened to me three times! It never worried me, but everyone else was terrified. When I finally got rid of it, it was ready to be junked."

Actress and comedian, LILY TOMLIN *presently owns two old banged-up Sevilles and a cherry-red '55 Dodge Royal Lancer.*

vanessa williams

"We had a little yellow Lancia—an Italian sports car. Everyone thought of it as my car, or it was going to be as soon as I could drive. One night, before I actually got my driver's license, my parents went out to a party or someplace. I decided I was going to take the car, pick up my friend and go to the movies. There was only one problem: the car had a stick shift, and I didn't know the first thing about shifting. But how difficult could it be?

"Anyway, I got to Nan's house and to the movie theater (*Hair* was great!), but on the way out of the parking lot, there was a steep hill we headed up. Of course, I had already shifted into third and had no concept of downshifting to get up a hill. So right there at the top of the drive, the car stalled. I broke into a sweat, started the car again and successfully got up that hill and all the way home.

> "There was only one problem: the car had a stick shift, and I didn't know the first thing about shifting."

"When I brought the car home at the end of the night, I had to figure out how to put it in reverse in order to park it the way I'd found it. I was there struggling with it for a long time. Finally, Mr. da Silva, our next-door neighbor, saw me and he knew I had no business being in that car. He helped get it back in place before my parents got home. But the next day, he went and told them. Of course, everyone assured them that I had been trying to get the car out of the driveway. They didn't know that I had taken that little, yellow Lancia all the way to Bedford Hills and back. They still don't know."

Former Miss America VANESSA WILLIAMS *is an actress, recording artist and the mother of two.*

"Upon being appointed an instructor at Harvard, I immediately went out and bought a car—first one. It was a 1953 Chevrolet convertible. I did not save any money for it and therefore had to buy it on the installment plan. My annual salary was $3,000 and the car cost $2,300.

"I remember that my future mother-in-law, knowing that I was courting her daughter, was worried that I was a spendthrift and made special inquiries about my character as a result of this extravagant purchase.

"My special memories about the car are of picking up my wife for our dates; she won a special place in my heart by polishing and Simonizing the car for me. I think this was the decisive factor in bringing about our marriage, which has successfully endured."

ZBIGNIEW BRZEZINSKI *is the former National Security Advisor to President Carter.*

zbigniew brzezinski

"We were a family, my mother, my two twin brothers and I, when we came to America from England during the war. We had nothing to lose and everything to gain. We felt very, very adventurous. My mother was a brave and wonderfully resourceful person. After all, she was an actress! She had just been on tour, traversing Canada with a show that was in aid of the Canadian RAF, and instead of going back to New York, she cashed in her ticket and stayed in Los Angeles. She wrote and told me that she had found some relatives who owned an apartment building on Ocean View Avenue in downtown Los Angeles in back of Bullock's Wilshire. At that time, we were living down in the Village in New York in a one-room apartment; to come to Los Angeles was a dream come true!

"When my brothers and I moved out to the coast, we were very hard up. My mother and I combined our earnings and bought a small Ford for all of $125, which I got to drive. It was a light creamy beige two-seater with a jump seat in the back, and it was an absolute dream car!

"We would pack picnics in the back, and the dog and the boys, who were going to school at the time. My mother and I sat in the front seat. And we would drive out to the beach. Los Angeles was quite a different place than it is today. It was a small town, and it seemed so much hotter in those days, hot and dusty. There was no humidity. And so to be able to drive along Sunset Boulevard and not have to take the Red car, which went on a track from Los Angeles to the beach, this really represented freedom. This car took us to the desert, which was exciting; it took us to the mountains, to Idlewild, up above Palm Springs. In other words, it was our link to being able to discover and enjoy the places in California, which otherwise we would have never been able to see. That car really spelled Freedom and Adventure."

ANGELA LANSBURY *is a star of television, stage and screen. Her second car was a DeSoto, which she bought after signing her first contract with* MGM.

angela lansbury

"It was a light creamy beige two-seater with a jump seat in the back, and it was an absolute dream car!"

paul rodriguez

"Let me tell you about that piece of junk: it was a black, beat-up '64 Corvair. I think the only reason I got it was because nobody in my family wanted it. It was actually my brother's car, a hand-me-down. It was basically up on blocks and didn't work. My brother suckered me into buying it. He said, 'Look, these cars are very dependable. You don't have to put any water in it. It's air-cooled.' Sure. And it was great on gas mileage because it would never run. It was always breaking down.

"It was a piece of junk, but like every teenager, I had to have a car. In my neighborhood, where I grew up, you had to have a car before you could have a girl. In Los Angeles, even to this day, if you don't have a car, you're not portable. For a teenager, a car is a symbol of your masculinity; especially among Chicanos, it's a big thing. The girls would always want to find out about you, but instead of asking, What's his name? or How tall is he? or How attractive? they'd want to know what kind of car you had. I knew big, fat, ugly guys with good-looking cars and good-looking girls. Me, I dated Juanita and Mary Alice, girls who were awfully ugly, and that was due to that damn Corvair.

"At the time, there were a lot of drive-ins in Los Angeles. But you couldn't even make out in a Corvair. I think there's more room inside a Yugo. And it was so low to the ground the people sitting in the car right next to you could look in and see what you were doing. So the girls would always say, 'No, not here.' I'd say, 'Well, what's a drive-in for?' I think that car was the reason I was a virgin until I was twenty-four.

"I didn't do any better after that because I got rid of that car and got a Pinto. So you can see I have great experience with cars. It wasn't until I went back to my roots and got me a Chevy that I got lucky."

PAUL RODRIGUEZ *is a comedian.*

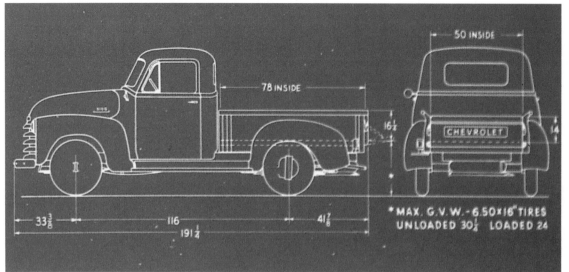

"My first car was actually a truck—a 1953 Chevrolet half-ton pickup. It was big and there was a lot of weight there. It was the old fifties style, very rounded; it had the big, wide white-walled tires on the sides. It sounds like a really strange choice, but my Uncle Mark was into car restoration, and he was the guy who got me interested. Right after I turned sixteen, he came over to the house with his new acquisition. It looked like a gardener's truck, all rusted and beat to hell, but I had seen other cars that my Uncle Mark had worked on, and I knew that it was going to be just a matter of months before this thing was gleaming. Even in that condition, I fell in love with it.

"After eight or nine months it took a major transformation and I had just about the hottest car in school. It never let us down, never broke down. All my friends' cars were breaking down left and right, but mine was just going strong. Since it was meant to be a farm truck, it was pretty much indestructible.

"I kept it for about three years and then I sold it to my uncle's best friend, who still has it. I sold it when I decided to switch from playing the drums to guitar. I sold my first car to buy my first guitar—a Jackson Electric."

Today, Gunnar Nelson owns a 1965 K convertible Mustang, a 1973 Detomaso Pantera, and a Harley Davidson. His fondest memories are of his faithful '53 Chevy—and he is currently attempting to buy it back.

"To me, it symbolized my freedom, freedom to move and progress. We had some pretty tough times at home around that time; we weren't getting along with our mom. There was a communication barrier going on. So I would basically point that car west, toward my friend's houses, and hang out there.

"It was a 1968 Mustang hardtop. I got it about seven months after my sixteenth birthday. I saved up for it by delivering pizza in a friend's car. It had belonged to a friend of my mother's, who had owned it since it was new. I bought it from him for $1,300, so it wasn't exactly a pristine example. There was a dent on the front valance panel, under the license plate, and I don't think that bumper was ever straight. But it was perfect for me, because aside from music, restoring cars is my passion. It was white with a Palomino interior, and all things considered, it went really fast. The great thing about it was that it was really comfortable, roomy on the inside and with a big backseat. I had a great girlfriend at the time, so we have plenty of fond memories of that car.

"I vowed that one day I'd get another one."

In addition to a 1966 427 Shelby Cobra, a Mercedes 190 16-valve and a Harley Davidson, MATTHEW NELSON *owns a 1965 Mustang GT convertible.*

"My memorable experience is one that every convertible owner has at least once, except in my case it was worse than usual."

liberace

"The car was a red convertible, an Olds 88—eighty-eight, as in the keys on a piano. The year was 1950. I was thirty-one years old. Before that, I couldn't have afforded a car of my own. I saved up and paid cash for the car. This was about two years before I went 'big time' with television.

"My memorable experience is one that every convertible owner has at least once, except in my case it was worse than usual. It was 1952, and the Hollywood scene was kind of new to me. I didn't know how easy it was to call a limo and play the big shot, so when I was invited to a very formal party, I took the convertible. I had become friends with Sonja Henie, the skater and actress, and we were going to get together. And on the way it started to rain and the top wouldn't go up. This very glamorous movie star and I arrived at the party looking like two sick, wet dogs.

"I kept the car until 1954, when one of our sponsors, a bank, gave me a custom-made Cadillac with piano keys on the seat covers and a candelabra as the hood ornament."

Legendary entertainer LIBERACE *was famous for incorporating his cars into his performances.*

john glenn

"My dad gave me a dilapidated 1929 Roadster when I was sixteen. It was a battered old car that I had painted bright red, and it had a canvas top that I always kept lowered. I named the car 'the Cruiser.' I was known as Bud at the time.

"My hometown is New Concord, Ohio, and it was a great place to grow up. I remember my friends would pile into the Cruiser for rides into the countryside or to the ice cream parlor, the Ohio Valley Dairy, on Main Street. My wife, Annie, and I had started going steady in the eighth grade, and always ordered either giant tubs of chocolate ice cream with marshmallows or giant hot fudge sundaes. The Dairy was a big place with large booths, always crowded with teenage kids. There was a jukebox that played the big-band hits. And it was actually a dairy: If you went around the back, you could see the cows grazing.

"Annie was included in virtually all of my activities with the Cruiser, except for an occasional exploit of derring-do. I had a fascination with speed, and I used to rev up the convertible, which was hardly a fast vehicle, to maximum speed and 'shoot' the old B&O Railroad bridge. It was a risky endeavor because the bridge was only the width of one car and quite steep, which made it impossible for me to see oncoming traffic until I was over the crest. One day I was taking the bridge at top speed, on the fly, just as another car was coming from the other side. We would have collided if the driver hadn't slammed on his brakes at the last minute and swerved out of the way. I stopped the practice after that."

JOHN GLENN *was the first man to orbit the planet Earth and is now a U.S. Senator from Ohio.*

"My dad had a variety of cars throughout my lifetime. He was always meticulous about keeping his cars serviced and polished and washed. At the age of ninety-two he still drives. He loved cars, and it just rubbed off on me.

"The first car I ever owned was a 1941 Plymouth convertible that my grandfather bought for me when I moved out here to L.A. It was an iridescent sand or gold or beige ragtop car. And I was absolutely nuts about it. You know, when you're a kid, that first car makes the biggest impression on your life. I went to high school in Chicago, but I finished my last year of high school out here in L.A. I was doing movies, I had a vocal group, I was an itinerant drummer, I was getting around town playing with a lot of groups, so that car served many functions.

"In those days, it was a much more innocent world. The world wasn't as permissive as it is now. Everybody went to the drive-ins, and by that I mean the food drive-ins. You'd get a malted and a hamburger and sit with your gal. It was a social event. That's what I remember in that car—going on dates with girls in L.A. and mainly enjoying not only the drive-in restaurants, but also the drive-in theaters, which were prevalent around here in those days.

"All the kids who had cars in California back then had what they called 'ripple disks'; they were large chrome hub caps and in the center was a strip, so when you drove, the strip turned around and flashed and looked great. My first real accessory with that car was a ripple disk.

"I had that car until 1947. God only knows what happened to it. I was doing very well, and I bought a brand-new Buick roadster. I guess we sold the Plymouth to someone out of the newspaper. I hated to see it go. It was, after all, my first car.

Singer MEL TORME *now owns a 1936 Jaguar 55 100, 1947 TC MG and a 1963 Rolls-Royce Silver Cloud— all of them polished and washed.*

stephen king

"It was a 1964 Galaxie. Sharp. I was about seventeen. I bought it from my brother for $250; he had gotten it as junk.

"I grew up way out in the country, in a place called Durham, Maine, and I lived seven miles from high school and seven miles from the place I worked after school and during the summer. Before this, after working the three-to-eleven shift at the textiles mill, I had to try to hook a ride with anybody who was going back—or else I'd have to thumb. I'd be standing out there and trying to look like, 'Sure, it's midnight, but I'm all right.'

"One very memorable, very embarrassing, experience was the time my car broke down in the middle of a bridge. In fact, I put that in one of my books. The needle valve froze, so when I had to get somebody stuck in *Cujo* I had that happen. The mill was getting off shift and people were piling up behind us and everybody was beeping and shouting things about my still being wet behind the ears. And 'Sell it for parts, kid!'

"It was a beautiful car. It had a bright red vinyl interior. Although I'm thinking, you know, this car would probably look like shit to me now. It's just in memory that it seems great."

STEPHEN KING *is a best-selling author. His second car was a 1956 Plymouth named Christine.*

"My first car was a '57 Ford Fairlaine hardtop convertible. It was mint green with a white top. I got it on December 1 in 1988. I had gone to L.A. to sing the National Anthem at the World Series and I was staying at the Hotel Mondrian. I looked out the window and across the street there was a car lot that specialized in antique cars. I called my mother and said, 'I found my car. I gotta go find out about it.'

"I went out and inquired about it and found out that it belonged to Julian Lennon. He's on the same label as I am, so I called some people from Atlantic and said, 'Maybe we can just do this thing directly.' In other words, 'Get me a better deal.' So they put me in touch with him, and he told me all the little things that were wrong with the car. It got shipped to New York, and it needed a lot of work. But I always said that I wanted a car that would turn heads and would make people say, 'What's that?' It did that, all right!

"I recently gave it away in conjunction with M.A.D.D., Mothers Against Drunk Driving. I gave it away at the Hard Rock Café, and the people who won it had to make the pledge not to drive it drunk. I thought it was good.

"You're gonna crack up when you hear what I replaced it with: a 1960 Thunderbird. Red."

Recording artist and songwriter DEBBIE GIBSON *is a car enthusiast.*

debbie gibson

mary kay ash

"The first pink Cadillac came about three years after we had started the company (Mary Kay Cosmetics). It came about because I went to the Cadillac dealer to purchase a new car and took along one of our little lip and eye palettes, which is a delicate shade of pink. I said to him, 'I want my car painted this color.' He looked at it and said, 'Oh, no you don't! Let me tell you how much it is going to cost you when that car gets here and you don't like it.' And I said, 'I want it pink. Please. Paint it pink.' And he said, 'Okay, but remember I warned you.'

"It came and actually created a sensation in Dallas! I'd drive up to an intersection and the waters would part. I'd get so much attention, and the people just loved it. Soon all our salespeople began to say, 'What would we have to do to get a pink Cadillac?' My son, Richard, is the person who takes care of all financial details, and I said to him, 'Take a pencil to this and tell me what it would take for someone to win one of these pink Cadillacs.' He did, and we set up the production requirements.

"The first year we gave one; the second year, five; the third year, ten; and after that, twenty. Then we opened it up so that any director who attained a certain amount of production wins a pink Cadillac to drive for a two-year period. There are actually three levels of winning—the first is the Pontiac Grand Am, which is red. Second level is a pink Gran Prix, and the third level is a pink Cadillac. The winners take excellent care of them because to them the car is a symbol of success. We call them 'trophies on wheels.' It turned out to be a wonderful marketing idea, however unexpected it was, because across the nation today we have $61 million worth of cars—that's about five thousand cars. From coast to coast, wherever you see a pink Cadillac, it is just automatically Mary Kay!"

MARY KAY ASH, *the founder and chairman emeritus of Mary Kay Cosmetics, still drives a pink Cadillac.*

"And I said, 'I want it pink. Please. Paint it pink.'"

"The first car I ever owned came a little late—I was twenty-seven years old, but I never had the money to own a car. I could barely keep myself in shirts and pants, let alone a car. When I went to the University of Iowa in 1961, I bought a car for $125. A Canadian Dodge. I remember the dealer said it was a Canadian Dodge, but to me it looked just like an American Dodge. I drove it for at least a year. I drove it as far as Nova Scotia and all over Iowa.

"It was essential to own a car in Iowa, especially during the summer, because it was so hot. Even the nights were hot...hot and damp. With a car you could go out on back roads at two or three in the morning and cool off. I think it was a two-toned car—maroon and gray. It had seen better days. One football weekend, it was parked on the street, and a drunk plowed into it. It was never right after that.

"It's not a very interesting story. I didn't save up for years to buy it. I didn't see it as an extension of myself. On the contrary; I saw it as a severe reduction of myself that *I* should be seen in something as lowly as this, this Dodge! I should be seen in a convertible!"

MARK STRAND *was the Poet Laureate of the United States. His second car was a Morris Minor with an Austin Healy engine, white with blue leather interior, and a convertible.*

"My first car was a white Ford, passed down to me by my mother. She paid $500 for it, and I had the car until I graduated from high school. I think one of the liveliest, lightest feelings I've had in my entire life was the way I'd feel, say, on my way to pick up a date, driving my first car. It was a feeling of being under my own steam. And feeling, you know, full of promise.

"I remember once, driving my teammates to a game, a baseball shoe got jammed under the brake and over the accelerator. The car was coasting, going fast, and it went even faster when I jammed on the brake. It kept going faster and faster until finally it rammed into the back of another car. I hit the car about four times before I realized what was happening. I could see the guy in front bouncing, flying up in the air. When we got out of the car, he was holding his back, and I thought I'd have him to take care of for the rest of my life.

"He promised he would be in touch, and I lived in fear for about a year. But it was a lucky car because, though I gave him my address and phone number, I never heard from him. I trust that he won't call now when he sees this."

Humorist Roy Blount Jr. *is a contributing editor to the* Atlantic Monthly *and* Spy, *and writes for many magazines.*

roy blount jr

richard condon

"In 1936, the year we were married and for reasons formed by deep national instincts, I bought a yellow 1933 convertible Chevrolet roadster. A roadster was a Del which has passed into history with the Jazz Age and the five-cent cigar. The car had a removable [leather], cushioned front seat in keeping with the standing folklore of the time which had a young man, carrying such a front seat under one arm, and supporting a young woman on the other, approaching a motorcycle cop on a rural highway saying, 'I want to report the theft of a car.'

"The yellow Chevrolet could seat two people comfortably under the canvas canopy of the driving compartment, and two avowed enemies in what is still chillingly known, to survivors, as the 'rumble' seat in the open air immediately behind them. The cockpit was a compartment for two, about as spacious as a torpedo tube in the first submarine. It had no roof or walls for protection from wind and weather, although in those days it was not a going thing for citizens to take potshots at passing cars with rifle or shotgun. At that time, for supple/nubile people under twenty-two, there was nothing more sporting or romantic than a rumble seat.

"The luxurious driver's compartment, with its pedaled floor, had no windows. 'Storm curtains,' made of rubber and ising glass, folded flat and snapped against the canvas roof of the compartment. Another possible drawback was the single nonelectric, dual windshield wipers.

"As I remember it, it rained a great deal more in those days than now that we have automatic windshield wipers, so, while handling brake, gear pedals and accelerator with one's feet, one steered the vehicle with one hand while alternately changing gears and frantically manipulating the manual windshield wiper with the other.

"The car cost $500. I have no recollection of where I found such an amount of money. I have blanked out on that part of the transaction, but I know I didn't have that kind of money. I was making $45 a week as a very junior copywriter at an advertising agency, having been jumped up from $10 a week for writing 'package inserts' for a lithographing company, those detailed folders printed in six-point type which no one ever reads but which, wrapped tightly around the product, explained the acana of such elixirs as patent medicines and scented lotions for growing hair. My parents didn't contribute any money to the purchase of a car although my father, who had built a rich vocabulary of vile oaths through the purchase of his first automobile, called a Metz, in 1922, scuffing his shoes badly as he kicked the car's tires, understood the male necessity for the car-buying ritual.

"Americans had to own cars because there were no driv-ur-self rental companies and because the oil companies had spent millions of dollars to lobby Congress and state legislatures to build roads and highways. These had to be used; by males, driving their own vehicles, inflicting upon American families from coast to coast the need for the cruel aberration called 'the Sunday drive,' which benefited not only the oil industry but plumbers everywhere because 'rest rooms' had to be installed for automobiling families having small children.

"My fiancée was no small factor in the purchase of the yellow Chevrolet with the rumble seat. She was certifiably glamorous; a Powers model; beauteous, uncluttered, with a disposition as soft as the down on angels' wings, instinctively understanding of male rituals, eleven of which she still is. She took it for granted, totally, that being a twenty-one-year-old American male that, as one signalling his arrival at a main station in life, that I had to buy that automobile. She knew, although the word would not be invented for almost twenty years, it would have been un-American not to buy the car. Further, at that time, gasoline was twelve cents a gallon.

"I was able to afford to drive the car for about three months. Garaging it in central Manhattan cost $30 a month. There was insurance. Undoubtedly, although I have mercifully blacked out on this, there were 'payments' because that was the American way. I had the upkeep of courtship. I had nearly had a nervous breakdown qualifying for a driver's license in midtown Manhattan. At the third try, my father, who had friends in high places at Tammany Hall, was able to arrange for the ultimate test to take place in Brooklyn. At last, I could drive my car even if I couldn't afford it, but that was the most American ritual of them all.

"I sold the car to be able to get married. It was a clean break. I passed over the executed registration papers, accepted the check and turned away. I have had about seventeen cars in six countries since then, but nothing at any price or anywhere outclassed that 1933 yellow Chevrolet."

RICHARD CONDON *wrote over twenty-five novels, including* The Manchurian Candidate *and* Prizzi's Honor.

branford

"Ed, my former manager, had a 280 zx Nissan. He was just starting to do well, so he bought a Peugot 505, and he was moving his operations from Boston to D.C. I was talking about learning how to drive a stick shift. He says, 'I have an old Nissan. Why don't you take it back to New York with you?' Great. So I spent two days in Boston, riding around, learning how to drive a stick. Finally I leave. I'm about forty minutes into the ride and suddenly a huge, torrential downpour hits. It's that kind of rain you can't see five feet in front of you. So then I turn on the windshield wipers and they don't work. That's when I start to notice that there's no molding on the window on the passenger side, so water is leaking into the car and all over me. The windows start to fog up. I turn something on and hot air blows through and it was like a blanket of mosquitoes covered the window. So I'm on this road, going forty miles an hour, all this water, the windshield wipers don't work and I'm driving this car in third gear. And a routine, four-hour trip took seven hours!

"I finally get to New York, and I park the car in front of my house. I get up the next day, it won't start. I mean, the third day I've got the damn thing, it won't start. So I bring it to the shop, and they say it's the starter. Two hundred

marsalis

and thirty-five dollars. Bang! Gone! Drive the sucker around for another month. It keeps stopping. Take it to the shop, they don't know what it is. It could be the alternator. It still stops. Then they say it may be the battery. They replace the battery and still it stops. And I'm calling Ed the whole while saying, 'Hey, this car is messing up!' And he says, 'Well, it never messed up on me, man. You must be doing something wrong.' This went on for five months. I had to replace all the parts. Everything!

"One day, I was on the Brooklyn Queens Expressway on the way to watch the Mets play, and there is a point at which it merges and goes from three lanes to one lane and then back again to three. Right in the middle of that one lane, it conked out. I got out of the car, and I pushed it over to the neutral zone, jumped off the bridge, called a taxi, went to Shea Stadium and just left that car sitting there. Never to be seen again.

"About eight months later, Ed calls me and says, 'Where's my car, man?'

"'You're joking. Right?' I say to him. 'It's somewhere on the B.Q.E.!'

"He tells me: 'It's a classic car!'

"And I say: 'Yeah. Right. Sure. It would have been with maybe $8,000 of work.'

"He says: 'Since you lost my car, I think I should be duly compensated.'

"I paid him, like, $100,000 for the car just so he would leave me alone. Then I got a new manager."

BRANFORD MARSALIS *is a saxophonist, composer and leader of NBC's The Tonight Show Band.*

Drawing by David Cowles originally in the New Yorker © 1989.

erma bombeck

"I did not have a first car. I mean, I didn't own one myself, not until I got married. In fact, we were married in 1949, and it was a whole year before we scraped together 150 big ones and bought a 1938 Plymouth. That's right, a 1938, black, four-door Plymouth. I wish I had it today. It was a terrible car.

"It had a gear shift, and I didn't know how to drive a gear shift, so my husband drove it. Everything on my side of the car was broken. The door was broken, the glass was broken, the glove compartment wouldn't close. Everything on his side of the car worked perfectly. That's the way we drove around for years. We had to carry water. We had to carry oil. When we would drive up a hill, we had a brick that we put behind the wheel so the thing wouldn't roll backwards. There was a lot of class to it.

"I have this picture of myself. I'm standing beside that car, wearing a hat and a dress. Why so dressed up in front of this dog, I'll never know. I suppose it's like having ugly bridesmaids at your wedding.

"Then, just before we got rid of it, my husband got everything fixed up. He just fixed that sucker up and it looked great. I can't remember, but we probably paid someone to take it off our hands. How else were we to clean up the country-side?"

ERMA BOMBECK *is a syndicated columnist and author of many books, including* When You Look Like Your Passport Photo, It's Time to Go Home.

"Why so dressed up in front of this dog, I'll never know."

hugh hefner

"It reminds me of the car Columbo used to drive."

"My first car was a 1941 Chevy Coupe that I bought in 1950. It cost about $400. It reminds me of the car Columbo used to drive. There's one experience I remember very well. I began *Playboy* in 1953. The first issue was undated, but it was actually a December issue that went on sale in November. I was still driving this car at the time, and the car finally quit in the middle of the street, the same day the magazine went on sale. I had a funny feeling when it happened. If the car could have talked, it would have said, 'You have to take it alone from here, pal.'"

HUGH HEFNER *is the founder of* Playboy.

jackie stewart

"The car I bought was an Austin A-30. I paid 375 pounds sterling. It was spruce green; it had Stewart Tartan seat covers in it; a Scotland badge on the side; and about twenty coats of polish before it was laid on the road. Because I couldn't drive until I was seventeen, I made sure that the car was delivered well in advance so that I could polish and prepare it for the great day.

"I couldn't sleep for days, or a week, or maybe it was three weeks even, beforehand. I sat my driver's test in that car, and fortunately passed. Then we were free to roam.

"Every day work finished, I went home, had a wash-up, a meal and then I went on the road. I was a spirited driver. I have to admit my youthful exuberance probably played an unfair part in terrorizing the local community.

"It was a great symbol of freedom to me, my car. The motor car, to this day, is the greatest form of independent choice of travel that exists in the world. It just gives one that independence. You know, until that time, like every young person, I depended on my parents to take me places, or friends coming to collect me to take me to see a film, or just to socialize.

"The car was also a very important thing for my romantic life. What better mode of romancing a young lady than a car? I think the car played an important part in many a romance. Young people today probably find more comfortable abodes to extend romantic lives than a motor car, but at that time no one had apartments or anything like that. The car was the mode of transport and the mode of romancing the lady in question. So I became quite athletic.

"I think we all, the human race, still have a love affair with the car. But I think we are rediscovering the car. Particularly in the United States in the past few years, it has tended to be a mechanical device for convenience, rather than for pride in ownership and mechanical excellence. Now I think that is beginning to change. I think more and more people in America are paying attention to the car, and I think the love affair is coming back. At least I hope it is. Oh yes, I still love the motor car as much as I ever did!"

Former race car driver JACKIE STEWART is a consultant for engineering research and development for the Ford Motor Company.

"It was a '64 Chevy II, a white wagon that I bought new when I was going to the University of Iowa. I was twenty-four years old, and I think the car cost $2,500. It's been my car, the car that I've driven, for many, many years. I've put the Chevy back together again. It's in great shape right now. The car has seen me through all kinds of times; it's always been there. The only time we were apart was when I went off to New York for about a year. But when I got back, I ran out to the garage and wham! we started right up again.

"One rainy day last year, however, the car skidded, the front tires went up an embankment, and then it just kind of g-e-n-t-ly turned over on its top like a turtle. I promise, the car didn't even block traffic. It was just perfectly parallel-parked against the side of a mountain. Going in the same direction, wheels still spinning. I wasn't hurt, but the Chevy was. I took it in, and just because I love it, I spent more to have it restored than I spent for it originally.

"I've bought a couple of cars for my wife, but I always drive the Chevy. I love it. There's a lot of me, and my life, in that car, and I wouldn't think of letting go of it. I don't suppose I'll ever get rid of it. I can't imagine what would replace it."

Recording artist
AL JARREAU
still drives his
Chevy II.

al jarreau

58

"I was born loving cars. I drove my first car when I was nine years old in Texas, where I was born and raised. We lived on a farm—not that we were farmers—but I used to drive out in a field where I could practice. I remember that car; it was a 1929 Dodge Touring.

andy granatelli

"The first car I ever owned wasn't very exciting. I mean, nothing compared to the cars that came later in life. I bought it for $35. It was a '31 Model A Coupe, and it hardly ran. I had to rebuild the whole car myself. I had to redo the transmission, the engine, the clutch, the kingpins, the brakes and the radiator. I had to do everything over. When it was all finished, I liked the car. I loved the car. I went on my honeymoon with that car. I have some fond memories of that car. Sure. Like making love in the front seat of that Model A Ford. You know how small the front seat of a Model A is? It was a great car."

ANDY GRANATELLI *is a race-car-driving great.*

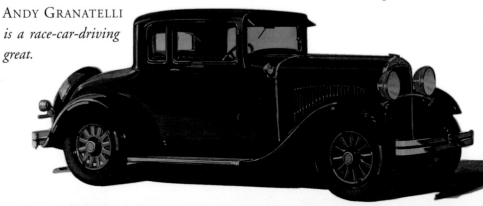

kelly lynch

"Steve McQueen was my hero, so what could it be? It was a 1969 gold Oldsmobile 442, with black interior, black convertible roof, dual exhaust, the classic square, square shape like the GTO had, an eight-track tape deck, Dylan and Elvis tapes, cool, a total Steve McQueen muscle car.

"It was a famous car in Minneapolis. They used to call it the Bitchmobile. I'd pile in all my girlfriends and we'd ride up and down the main drag, singing along with Nancy Sinatra, hanging out of the car and yelling to everyone. Can you picture it, all these screaming blondes terrorizing the town and driving all the guys crazy? They were too terrified of us. Car-o-Bitches! It was a summer car. In Minneapolis there was nothing better than to have one of these muscle cars, top down, cruising around town. But in the winter it was another story. It took hours to thaw. I'd drive to my little

> **"They used to call it the Bitchmobile. I'd pile in all my girlfriends and we'd ride up and down the main drag, singing along with Nancy Sinatra, hanging out of the car and yelling to everyone."**

job at the mall in the ice and snow, and hear the cracking of the convertible too. It was too sad. Eventually I sold it to a mechanic.

"I still think muscle cars are the only cool things to drive. I own one now. A classic 1964 Chevy Malibu S.S., candy-apple red. Whenever I do a fashion shoot, I always try to be photographed with my car. You see, all my life I wanted to be the Chevy girl."

KELLY LYNCH *is a model and actress who appeared in* Drugstore Cowboy.

tom wolfe

"I've only owned two cars in my life, although I love driving. I bought the first car in order to have a job on a newspaper—my first job. It was 1956, and I was a citywide reporter for the *Springfield Union* in Springfield, Massachusetts, and you had to have a car. So I bought a 1953 Ford Country Squire station wagon; why, I don't know.

"It was one of the last station wagons that had wood on it. It had metal sides with big strips of wood; today they do the same thing, but they make them out of fiberglass. It constantly grew mushrooms out of the wood. It would get wet, and I didn't have anyplace to put it: I had no garage or anything. It would get wet and these mushrooms would grow and grow. It was a very strange car.

"I bought the car in '56; it was four years old when I bought it, and I kept it until 1962, when I came to New

York. I took it to Washington and used it while I was working on the *Washington Post*. I used to park it on the street all the time. I always left the doors unlocked so that anybody who wanted to break in wouldn't have to break anything. However, a car with mushrooms growing out of it was not a prime target.

"I traveled a lot in it. It broke down once. I was traveling from Washington to Long Island for my summer vacation. It was 105 degrees that day, and the car broke down on the New Jersey Turnpike at Union City. I was so hot I remember sitting by the side of the Turnpike; I don't know why, but I had a black umbrella, and I was eating cucumbers. I also don't know why I brought the cucumbers along, although I knew cucumbers had water in them, and it was really hot.

"They towed the car, with me in it, into Union City. And Union City, at least the part where they repaired cars, was the most woebegone, broken-down town you've ever seen in your life. They said it was going to take two or three hours to fix, so I started wandering around. And I came to understand the Catholic Church in a way. There was, in the middle of this rotting section of town, an absolutely stunning stone cathedral. I knew that a stone building would be cool, so I went inside.

"The place was absolutely majestic. There were a few people inside lighting votive candles, going by the Stations of the Cross, and so on, and I thought to myself, Isn't it just great to have something like this, so that no matter what your circumstances—such as being homeless and adrift beside the Jersey Turnpike—you have this absolutely majestic place to go to that in some way is yours. I was raised a Presbyterian, and Presbyterians don't build structures like that. It's against our religion, actually.

"I think the Lord must have been watching, or I went to the right church perhaps, because they only charged me $35, and I had thought I was going to be taken and just depleted. However, it was the beginning of my vacation, and I had $35 with me. I used to travel for five hundred miles with $12 in my pocket because that was more than enough for gasoline. When you're young, as long as you have three or four extra dollars for sandwiches—then you don't worry. It's great to feel that immune to things. I did love that car."

TOM WOLFE *is a journalist and novelist. He is the author of many books, including* The Right Stuff *and* The Bonfire of the Vanities.

pee-wee herman

"At the time, I wouldn't have taken any amount of money for it. It was my first car. It was a really, really big deal! A Rambler Nash, silver, and it had that kind of nubby material on the seats. It also had a radio, which I thought was really cool! But the neatest thing about the car was that the seats went all the way back, so you could actually sleep in it, which I did!

"Actually, I bought the car before I got my license. I remember because I was disqualified during my driver's test in that car. We buckled up and started to leave the test area, when the instructor said, 'Everything all right? You sure you don't want to check everything one more time?' 'Okay,' I said, and I checked everything again. He said, 'Start.' After I drove about twenty yards, he said, 'All right, stop the car! Your emergency brake is on and that disqualifies you!'"

PEE-WEE HERMAN's *vehicles of choice are bicycles and scooters. He is qualified to drive both.*

"But the neatest thing about the car was that the seats went all the way back, so you could actually sleep in it, which I did!"

"The first car I had was an old wreck, a Ford Pinto. My father bought it from one of the partners in his law firm. He paid $100 for it. It was four or five years old at that point and very beat up. I was seventeen. My parents had it painted orange before they gave it to me. I drove it around almost three years, and then sold it for about $50 to some people my parents knew. Their son drove it another years.

"My next car, which I bought myself, was a Mercedes 450 SL."

Winner of about every tennis award including three time Wimbledon champ and four time U.S. Mens Singles champ, JOHN MCENROE *is considered to be one of the greatest players of the game.*

john mcenroe

"My kids are all very close in age, so when they were growing up I started making toys for them. I'd make little cars, just little rinky-dink things. When they started going to birthday parties—which seemed like every week—I started making them these cars to take as presents. Then I'd go to the kid's house, and I'd notice the piece was sitting up on the fireplace or in a cupboard someplace. And I'd say, 'How come the kid doesn't have the toy?' And the mother would say, 'Well, I'm going to give it to him when he's older and he can appreciate it.' But they were meant to be played with! I always made them so they could be played with. I remember Dad talking about the Buddy-El cars and toys he used to have in the thirties. I've seen pictures of them, and kids *played* with them.

"The first car I made was kind of a roadster. It looked very homemade. I really hadn't pushed on it. Not like what I do now. But, at the time, it was a monumental work for me, and it took me months to do it. Now? Now I put a lot of work into these things, but I still always make them so that if you really wanted to lie down on the floor and play with this car, you could do it. And I know guys who do it. My neighbors think I'm nuts, because I make a car and I'm out in the yard playing with it. I like to play with toys."

BRUCE CRAWFORD *is a master builder of model cars; his first full-sized car was a 1956 Nash Metropolitan.*

bruce crawford

I haven't really learned how to drive yet.

-but-but-but-

So techically, you'd have to say my first car was the one my parents owned when I was small.

It was a 1954 Chevrolet with a blue body and a white roof.

Its name was "Bluebell."

Now, where'd I park Bluebell?

One of its most curious features was a rope that went all the way across the back of the front seat.

Since I always sat in the back, I guess I had a pretty constant view of it.

My folks explained that it was for hanging up things one retrieved from the dry cleaners~

a situation that occurred about once a year in our family.

If I wash this suit by hand, we can save ten dollars!!!

Nonetheless, I always thought of it as the dry cleaning rope.

CAR MANUAL
CHEVROLET 1954
fig. 1-A

DRY CLEANING ROPE

Sometimes it reminded me of the reins on a horse~

~supposedly there to steady the rider, but actually of no use whatsoever.

AAAAAARGH

In any case, in 1963, Bluebell was replaced by a more fully functioning, though ropeless, black Rambler.

Roz Chast is now learning to drive.

69

dan rather

"My first car was a badly used and abused 1939 Ford. I bought it in 1952, when I was twenty-one years old. Went in half-ers with my college roommate, Cecil 'The Weeper' Tuck, with the money I'd earned over the summer as a brush cutter for a pipeline crew. We bought the car from a used-car lot on the outskirts of Houston. All four tires blew and the clutch went out as we nursed it the eighty-five miles from where we bought it to the campus at Huntsville, Texas. We repaired the clutch insofar as it could be repaired—in the dark, in the rain, alongside a road near Conroe. We named the car 'the Thing.' The Thing became the talk of the town, partly because the brakes were constantly going and partly because it crashed into several campus buildings, including the women's dormitory."

DAN RATHER *is the anchorperson for the* CBS Evening News.

"In the summer of 1988, I had the lead role in a film (*Short Circut II*) and I decided to buy my first car. The day the film was released, I was in L.A. and I was walking down the street. I saw this 1963 Mercury Comet convertible, and I thought, Now, that is incredible. But there was no For Sale sign on the window or anything. So I knocked on the guy's door and I said, 'You wanna sell this car?' He said, 'No. No, I don't.' Then I said, 'You sure you don't wanna sell me your car?' He said, 'Wait a minute. I'll sell it, but only for one price—$3,500.' I said, 'Yeah, I'll buy it,' and we arranged it. He was shocked. He didn't know he could get that much for it and

fisher stevens

he'd had no intention of selling it. We arranged a meeting place and I brought him the money. As I pulled away, he started crying. He waved to me. The car was in mint condition, it was beautiful, it even had his name on the license plate. STAN. I felt like I knew this guy because I had his car, and I was starting to feel like maybe I shouldn't have taken it. I mean, I'm the kind of guy that makes more of a wreck of a rent-a-wreck. I can't park, that's my big problem. And the car had these little fins. Every time I would park I would hit these fins and it was kind of a disaster.

"Then I got this urge to get out of Los Angeles, and the only way to get out was to drive across country in my car. I got this mechanic to give it a tune-up, and he said, 'DO NOT, whatever you do, DO NOT take this car across country. DO NOT. It will never make it.' But I had to take it.

"My girlfriend at the time and I, we decided to drive to New Orleans, and then I would continue on to New York with my friends Patrick, Charlie and Matt. Well, on the second day of our journey, we got into a desert. Sign said: Gas Station, 40 Miles. After about thirteen miles the car started to make unbelievable noises. *Prrcchh. Prrcchh! Prrcchh!* I thought this was the end for us. Then, an unbelievable thing happened—we saw a cardboard sign that said, MIKE THE MECHANIC. It was handwritten in black crayon. It's this yard in the middle of nowhere, pieces of amusement park rides, and some huge storage tank that Mike had cut a door into and was using as a living room.

"Mike found that one of my spark plugs was blown. He replaced it, said we might have problems, so we bought a lot of spark plugs to take with us. This guy Mike, he was our hero. We even built a little shrine to him on the side of the road.

"Basically, we broke down thirteen or fourteen times before we got to New Orleans. Then on to Graceland, to Memphis, Wayne, West Virginia, the Adirondacks, where we met a one-legged mountain climber, and then finally New York. We actually made it across the country.

Actor FISHER STEVENS *still owns his first car. It follows him wherever he goes.*

62 LINCOLN CONTINENTAL

"When I was working for *Saturday Night Live*, we were all sitting around with Ricky Nelson, who was the guest host that week. Somehow, we all got talking about our first cars. Mine was a big junk heap. Everybody else's was pretty much like that too. Then Ricky Nelson said, 'Well, mine was a '55 T-Bird.' You could almost hear it click in everybody's head, 'AH! Ricky Nelson. I get it.' You see, we'd forgotten who we were talking to. *Of course* he would have owned the dream car we all would have given our left nut for.

"My car was a '56 Buick, a big beast of a car with a name like Roadmaster or something, but I got it in '65 so the thing was really used. For a hundred dollars, you can imagine what a good car it was. The best thing about it was a Stromberg Nelson radio that could pull in stations from the moon. But I still have a good feeling about it. To me, it meant what a car always means—freedom. I happen to like big cars. I currently own a '62 Lincoln Continental, the second largest car ever made in America. The wonderful thing about big cars is that there's a lot of metal between you and the maniac. And you could fool around in them, neck in them. These cars had backseats where you didn't have to go through some contortionist thing to get laid."

MICHAEL O'DONOGHUE *is a co-founder of* The National Lampoon *and former head writer for* Saturday Night Live.

michael o'donoghue

"I didn't get my own car until I was seventeen. The year was 1957. I was living with my first husband in Schenectady, New York, and the hottest ticket back then was a 1940 Ford Coupe. I wanted one badly and finally found one in a barn in the middle of nowhere. I bought it for $40. My husband gave it a paint job, and he also replaced the engine with a Cadillac V-8.

"I started racing the Ford from red light to red light, and I don't ever remember being beaten. I was the top dog—that car became real famous. People came from miles around to race me, but they never won. And I was the only woman racing on the streets then. Guys didn't like losing to me much, but they learned to live with it. And yeah, I got a few speeding tickets—we'd hit up to 120 miles per hour.

"I sold the car in 1958 to get a Chevy. I couldn't afford both cars. Now I have a 1982 Mercedes station wagon and 1990 Lincoln Mark VII."

SHIRLEY MULDOWNEY *was the first woman to compete for a National Hot Rod Association championship in a top fuel dragster. She won the competition in 1980 and again in 1983. The movie* Heart Like a Wheel *was based on her life.*

"In high school we had vocation days where they would give us stacks of pamphlets and folders about various occupations that would be sure to keep our culture and economy going. At the time, I wanted to be a race car driver for a Ferrari team. I had to make up my own pamphlets because they weren't offering that as a vocation. I was this Wasp. I was supposed to go on to banking and business. But from thirteen to seventeen, I was fascinated with stock car racing. I had sound recordings of the races; I'd sit and listen to them for hours, identifying the different cars by the sound of their motors revving...

spalding

'That's a Mazzeratti...that's a D'Jag!' I don't know where this fascination came from. I suppose it had to do with the fact that I was reaching puberty, and I didn't have a girlfriend; it was a sublimated desire.

"But the first car I ever had was a '37 Plymouth that I bought from a neighbor. A black coupe, two-door, stick shift. My friend Fred Bodell and I drove it to his house on Poppasquash Point in Bristol, Rhode Island. He and his family lived on one hundred acres. He had a clamshell driveway more than a mile long, and it had a hairpin as you came up to the house. We drove the Plymouth from Barrington to Bristol, which is about fifteen miles. I had no license. I was fourteen. We got there, and it was all overheated, smoke was pouring out from under the hood. The guy had sold it to me with no oil, and I was furious with him. As soon as Fred and I got there, we tore the muffler off and ran a piece of plex pipe under the running board. We couldn't stop driving up and down that driveway with flames shooting out from the bottom of the car just like at the stock car races. We were taking that hairpin curve, sliding on the clamshells, these two other friends riding the running board like crazy Keystone Cops. I don't know why we weren't killed. When Fred's parents came home, they were happy he was with me and not with those Portuguese Bristol gangs who all wore motorcycle jackets and were up to no good.

"Yes, I remember the smell of the inside of that car—the old fuzz, tuck-and-roll upholstery, the crank windows, the blue discolored windshield, two-door, floor shift, black bomb.

"At last, my whole racing career ended in Bristol. When I got my license, I took the family car down Colt's Drive with a friend. It was a '53 two-toned, royal blue-and-gray Ford with an automatic transmission which drove me crazy. I only wanted to drive cars with stick shifts. But I was fantasizing that I was road-racing with the Ferrari team, doing laps on Colt's Drive on a rainy day in September. The car spun on wet leaves and rolled over, and we ended up against the seawall. If it had gone any further we would have been killed. When I came to, the car was on its side, and my friend was using my body as a ladder to climb out. I reached over and turned off the radio. My friend said, 'If my mother knew I was out in this rain she'd kill me.' Neither of us had ever been in shock before, so we didn't know we were in shock. He looked at me and said, 'You've got blood running down your head.' We got to the National Guard Station on Colt's Drive and called my father. He drove down from Barrington to pick us up, to look over the car, and to see how badly it was damaged. When he got home, my mother asked him, 'What did it look like, dear?' He said, 'Like the two boys in it should be dead.' I never knew if he meant that it was lucky we were alive or if he was so angry he'd rather we were dead. After that, my racing career slowed down, and I began driving like my grandfather."

Actor and storyteller SPALDING GRAY *now owns a 1969 Rambler.*

ronald reagan

"My first car was a new 1934 Nash. I dreamed about one long before that of course. I remember when I worked as a lifeguard and my boss, Ruth, used to pick me up every day. When I got the car, I was working as a sports announcer at WHO radio in Des Moines, Iowa. I'd gotten that job on a tip from someone I'd met while I was in Chicago. I remember all the hitchhiking and the sore, swollen feet. I couldn't afford taxis, and I was afraid to ride the buses. The city itself scared me out of my wits. Everybody seemed to know where they were going, and I could have gotten lost looking for a men's room.

"But it is of my second car, a Ford convertible, that I have my fondest memories. In 1937 Warner's offered me a contract: seven years, with a yearly option, starting at $200 a week. Of course I accepted immediately, before they had a chance to change their minds.

"The contract was dated to begin June 1, and how well I remember, early one morning toward the end of May, heading west in the pride of my life, my first convertible. I remember crossing the burning desert, and at sundown, driving that long stretch between banked orange trees from San Bernadino to Los Angeles. I remember the fragrance of the orange blossoms, now replaced by smog.

"I remember how the old convertible helped me get one of the most important acting roles of my career. I had read the announcement in *Variety* that Warner's was planning to film the biography of Knute Rockne. For years I'd wanted to play the role of George

Gipp. I went to see the producer, who was very gracious, but it was clear he had no intention of even considering me for the role. In his view, I wasn't the type.

"Without another word, I dashed out of his office, headed for my car, and broke a few speed limits getting home. I found some old college football pictures, broke the same speed limits getting back, barged into his office, and slapped the pictures down in front of him. You know, most fellows look like football players in the suit. He asked if he could hang on to the pictures. I headed home, driving slower, because it's hard to hold a steering wheel with all your fingers crossed.

"I hadn't been back in the house fifteen minutes when the phone rang. It was a call from casting; eight A.M. shooting the next morning, testing for the part of George Gipp.

"When I'd been at Warner's a few years, I bought myself another convertible: this one was a Cadillac."

RONALD REAGAN *was the fortieth president of the United States.*

Excerpted in part from RONALD REAGAN'S OWN STORY by Ronald Reagan with Richard G. Hubler, by permission of the publisher Hawthorn/Dutton © 1965.

"My heart still pounds. It was a '58 red Chevrolet Impala convertible. It was used, and we got it in 1961 or '62. I thought it was the most beautiful thing on the face of the earth. I felt like I was king of the road. But in the Beverly Hills High parking lot, it was on the low end of the scale. This was the ultimate beach-wagon, and while I never board-surfed (I body-surfed), I had friends who did and we would unzip the rear plastic window and their boards would stick out the back.

"In retrospect, it seems a very racy car. At the time, it just seemed like normal transportation. A lot of cars have come and gone in my life since, but I don't recall ever having any trouble with that first car. I wonder what has happened to car manufacturing in this country that we can't get it right. Stupidly, I was convinced by my parents when I was graduating from high school in '63, and was going on to U.C.L.A., to get rid of that car and get a new one. I think Father bought me a '63 or '64 Chevrolet, and it just wasn't the same. It just wasn't right. I knew it wasn't as beautiful, but those were the days when you just got a new thing. I later hated myself for it. I don't know what happened to that '58 Impala. It's probably alive and well in Mexico."

A highly distinguished pianist, MISHA DICHTER *is hoping for a '58, red Impala convertible when he turns sixty.*

misha dichter

"Like all kids in high school, I desperately wanted a car, but I didn't need one. I grew up in Mississippi. In a small town you walk everywhere you want to go, you get there in jig time. You get used to that. Then as a teenager, I had a bicycle; then I was gone—I was in the service. A lot of guys in the service had cars and, of course, I always befriended somebody who had a car.

"I had been working for about eight months at the Los Angeles City College for $60 a week. Gross. I saw this car in a lot for $500. It was a 1952 white Ford convertible. I managed to get a down payment, and I bought it, and there I was in wheels. Life changed. It was like day and night. Without a car, I couldn't get a date. Then when I got a car, I turned 'em down.

"I remember once I was going out with some friends. We were going to the Moulin Rouge on Sunset. I had too much to drink, it was my car, and I was driving. I thought, I'm fine, I'm just terrific, I can do this. I was so sure of myself, so positive that I had everything under control. Well, I got into the parking lot at the Moulin Rouge and ran right into the side of a bus with my car. I didn't damage the car. It was a 1952 car, and they made 'em out of good stuff then. But I didn't drink and drive anymore after that."

The original Easy Reader on television's Electric Company, MORGAN FREEMAN *went on to become an Academy Award winner for* Driving Miss Daisy.

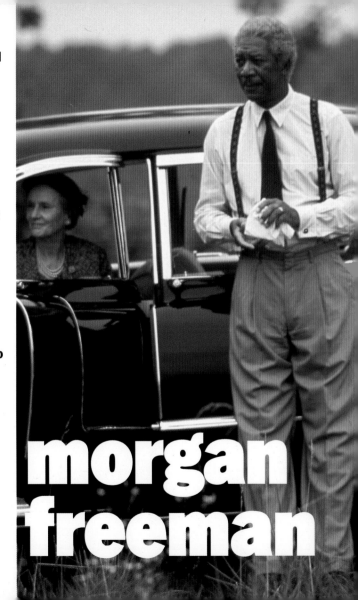

morgan freeman

dr. joyce brothers

"Let me tell you about my first car. I was married thirty-nine years; my husband died two years ago. All through our marriage, cars meant a great deal to my husband. He would shop for them and compare them and look and dream and read all the magazines and know everything there was to know. Cars didn't mean that much to me. I used to use my parents' cars before we were married, and when we got married, each new car that I owned was his castoff when he found a new love. Whenever I inherited one of his cars, it hated me on sight. It behaved like a pussycat for my husband, but as soon as it was mine it would fall apart and I would have problems like being on the roadside broken down and the only person stopping to help was a Hell's Angel, a biker with tattoos and bare arms and a leather vest. It was terrifying to see one of them walk up to you, but they were the only ones who would stop on the road to help. But I must say, they were the most helpful people ever.

"One time I got stuck in one of my husband's cars on the approach to the George Washington Bridge. There had been an unexpected snowstorm and I didn't have boots, I didn't have any covering for my head. I trudged up the approach to the bridge, which is about a quarter of a mile, in hip-deep snow to a help phone. I got on the help phone and said I was stuck on the approach to the George Washington Bridge. He said, 'What's your name?' I said, 'Joyce Brothers.' And he said, 'Stop kidding, lady,' and hung up!

"That was the end for me of my husband's cars. I bought a new one, the first and only car I owned myself up until that time. I bought one of those little Volkswagen bugs. The champagne edition convertible, white inside, white outside, and you could put the top down. It was the closest thing to peddling that you could get.

"Then I decided that I would do a very Hollywood thing and I bought my husband a Porsche for his birthday. The car was delivered on his birthday with a big red bow, and it was wonderful. But I was never allowed to drive that car. And once again I inherited his old car. His car was so much better than the Volks; it was safer, had more voom. At this point I sold the Volks. That was a sad thing, because I would watch it in the used-car lot. It had a little flag on it that said 'Special,' and the flag was always drooping, and I always felt so bad. But somebody bought it and they bought such a darling little car. So that was the love. And I haven't fallen in love since then."

DR. JOYCE BROTHERS *is a well-known author and psychologist.*

"I haven't owned a car for over twenty-five years. I've only owned one car—a beat-up white 1949 Studebaker. Oh, yes, I enjoyed cars. I had a typical teenager's interest in them. I'd love to buy another one—if the auto companies met certain standards of safety, efficiency and pollution control. One reason that I don't own a car is that I don't want it construed as a product endorsement. My line for praising cars would be if it had a sixty-mile-an-hour, fixed-barrier collision-protection level, which is what all cars should have. In other words, if people strike an abutment or a tree at sixty miles per hour, they should walk away uninjured, and we're a long way from that."

RALPH NADER *is a consumer advocate who has worked tirelessly on behalf of the driving public.*

ralph nader

From an advertisement for the 1948 Studebaker.

joan rivers

"I was living at home in Larchmont, which was a very affluent neighborhood. My father was a doctor, so there was a Mercedes and a Cadillac in the driveway. Then there was this wonderful, old 1958 Buick that my aunt had given me. It was broken down and so old and rusty. The tires were pathetic; they were put together with chewing gum. But it was *my* car.

"My mother used to say, 'Please don't park that car in front of the house.' If it was parked, it was towed, because they could never conceive of anyone in the area owning a car like that.

"But it was a very dear car to me. Larchmont is about twenty-odd miles from New York, and that car enabled me to drive in and back to Greenwich Village every night to perform in the comedy clubs. This was when I was just getting started.

"There was no floor on the right side—absolutely rotted away. I bought one of those Rubbermaid kitchen mats, and all my girlfriends sat with their legs up on that bump along the center of the floorboard. They could never put their legs down or they would've fallen through. But it worked very well. I had reverse and drive. I never had first or second. At the end, the drive went and all I had was reverse. I left it somewhere along the West Side Highway in New York, and everyone said, 'How could you leave it? They'll strip it!'

There was nothing to strip. I came back and added things to it."

JOAN RIVERS *is a comedian, author and television talk show host.*

james belushi

"My mom worked in the drugstore from nine to twelve. I'd ride to work with her, go in, get a pack of cigarettes, and then I would go and steal her car. I had a dupe key. She had a Galaxy 500 red-interior convertible. I would pick up my friends, go joy-riding and bring it back at quarter to twelve. I'd come in the drugstore and say, 'Mom, I'll drive back home with you.' I did that for years. I was about thirteen. I used to dress for it: I wore a hat, a sport coat and a phone book.

"I love cars. My only problem was that once I was old enough to own cars, I always owned beaters. But the one good thing about owning beaters is that you get to learn a lot about cars because you're always replacing the alternator, the cellenoid, the brakes, the muffler. Why, I can fix a muffler with a Coke can and a hanger and duct tape real good. I've done it many times. Also tires. I'm an expert on tires. I used to go behind gas stations at night and get the tires they'd thrown out during the day. I was constantly replacing tires on my first car.

"My first car was bought by my father for me. It cost $400. I think I was sixteen. It was an Oldsmobile 88. Tan outside. Tan interior. Had a radio that worked. The thing about that car was that you could fit nine people in it. It was a concert car. We saw the Allman Brothers, the James Gang, Mountain, Fleetwood Mac, the Allman Brothers, the Allman Brothers, the Grateful Dead. I was the driver. One night we were cruising around with a lot of people, and remember that song 'Hooray for Hazel'? That song came on the radio and for some reason we laughed so hard we named the car Hazel. Hooray for Hazel, 'cause Hazel got us around.

"She was a beauty. I loved her. Hazel.

"I remember how she died. I was delivering pizzas. The only way I could get that job was if I had a car. I said, 'Well, sir, I have a car.' You know, winters in Chicago are tough on old people and cars. A lot of people don't make it though the winter, and a lot of cars don't either. Well, Hazel, her transmission went on me with six pizzas in the back. Ten o'clock on a Saturday night. I just hung out until someone gave me a ride back to a pay phone. And you know what? I just left her there. I never saw her again."

JAMES BELUSHI *is an actor.*

"I was living in Beverly Hills when I turned sixteen, so I was a Beverly Hills High School student. It was a little embarrassing because everybody else had Mercedeses and Porsches, and I had a Capri—a light blue, '74 Capri. Anywhere else it would have been something great, but there it was nothing and no one cared about me. I definitely loved that car. A sunroof, stick shift—what more could a sixteen-year-old ask for? It meant I didn't have to walk and take the bus anymore. And in Physical Education, we had different activities like sailing, bowling, ice skating that involved leaving the campus. Having your own car meant you got to fill your car up with your friends, and the girls that you liked, you made them sit with the stick shift between their legs. This was definitely better than taking the bus.

"Later, that car was my ticket to New York. Selling it helped to pay for my plane ticket and my first month's rent on an apartment in New York. I was really sad to sell it; you get to know a car. It was like saying good-bye to a friend. Her name was Carey Capri. She was a big deal.

"The Cadillac was my second car. When I began to make money I was offered this car, and I decided to buy it. It was like a dream to have this Cadillac, because I was just beginning to customize 'things.' The car was the ultimate appliance."

Artist KENNY SCHARF *lives in Miami Beach and now drives a van.*

"The first car that I paid for was a 1950 Nash. It was pea green. It had four-wheel drive, which was kind of unusual in those days, and it looked like a tank. I bought it in St. Louis in 1959 for $75. It had 125,000 miles on it. Anne and I [his wife and fellow actor, Anne Meara] were working for the Compass Players, which was the predecessor to Second City. We were working at the Crystal Palace with Nancy Ponder and Alan Arkin, and we were just learning about improvisation. I bought the Nash so we could get back home to New York. It got me not only to New York, it got me to Palm Beach, Florida, then it got me to Chicago in 1960, and from there it got me to L.A.

"At this point, Anne and I were pregnant, and we were going to drive the car from L.A. back to New York. We had a few bucks in our pockets, because we had been working for six months steady for the first time in our life, so we decided to stop off in Las Vegas to gamble. This car was taking us out of Las Vegas and when we were right in the middle of the desert, outside a town called Winnemucca, the car started to steam up. We called the gas station in Winnemucca and some guy came and towed us in. He took one look at Anne, who was out to her sixth month of pregnancy, and said, 'You blew a gasket. We're gonna have to get you a new one. Might take two or three days.'

"The only place we could stay was in a South Pacific Railroad stopover, and there were no doors on the hotel rooms. These men, these train men, motormen, engineers and firemen, were running up and down the halls all night while we were lying in our bed. Next day we went looking for a better hotel. I asked the guy at the gas station when the gasket was going to arrive. He said maybe the next day. The next day came, but the gasket still hadn't arrived. I said, 'How far away do you have to send for this thing?' He said, 'Oh, about thirty miles.'

"'Can't you just go down there in a car and get it?'" I asked him.

"'Yeah,' he says. 'We could do that.'

"'Well,' I said. 'Why don't you?'

"'We like you people,' he said to us, 'and we just want you to hang around for a couple of days.'

"I got on a Greyhound bus, went to the parts place myself, and brought back the gasket. It took another day for them to put it in. We started out again, and after we had gone about ten miles into the desert, the thing blew again. The only way I can describe the feeling I had about this car that had taken me from St. Louis to New York to Palm Beach, to California and from California to here, was that I felt like I wanted to shoot it with a gun, like an animal that you love. I just wanted to put it out of its misery. That was the most beloved of all my cars. After that, nothing could top it.

"A couple of months ago, Anne and I were on the QE II, doing our show, and we arrived in Madras, India. There on the streets of India, every car is an Ambassador, and they are replicas of the car I had. They were all Nashes. I felt so at home riding in India with this car I almost went crazy. I said, 'I'm home again!'"

JERRY STILLER is an actor, writer, comedian and the husband of Anne Meara.

martin landau

"I guess it was in the early fifties or the late, late forties. Yes, it must have been 1949. I was still living in Brooklyn, where I'd grown up and gone to school. I bought a 1931 Chrysler convertible. It was a bit of a relic then—close to twenty years old—with two huge spare tires that sat in the front fenders, a convertible top that you could push back by hand. It had those S-bars on the side and it sat two comfortably in the front and two in the rumble seat. It had a crank, which I kept in the bottom of the rumble seat in case the car stalled or wouldn't start. And it bore the original paint job—a beautiful beige color with a beige top. I drove it everywhere.

"I remember one summer I went away to summer stock at a theater on Peak's Island, Maine. I had already had the car for two years. When I got back in September of that year, the car was sitting in front of the house and it was bright red. My friends—and I use that word with caution—painted my car fire-engine red while I was gone. I don't know if they thought this was a joke, a surprise or a present. Whatever it was it was not the best paint job in the world. I was furious. They had painted it with brushes! Bright, bright red! And, of course, they were gleefully watching my reaction, which amounted to horror. I hated what they had done.

"I kept it for a couple of months after that, and then I sold it for $75. I'd bought it for $95, and I certainly got $20 worth of use out of it. It would be worth many thousands today, even with that terrible paint job."
Actor MARTIN LANDAU *has owned a variety of cars since then—none of them are red.*

"My first car sat in the middle of a field. It had no tires, but was happy to run on its rims. It had no gear shift—it was a Model T—so shifting gears meant pushing down on a lever with your foot, which, if it stuck after the car started moving, made it prudent to move your foot away from it as quickly as possible because on release it had a kick like a mule. Its upholstery consisted of springs adorned by wisps of weather-eaten leather and stuffing.

"This was my first car, and I was nine years old playing a theater somewhere in the Midwest; and I had been lucky enough to make friends with the theater manager's little girl, who was my age. She and her friends, in describing this treasure to me, had omitted all of the above details, simply telling me that there was a car which belonged to her little group of friends, and that whoever came up with enough money for a gallon of gasoline could own it. I was thrilled. I gathered my pennies, we bought a can of gasoline, and the little group began the trudge toward the field.

"I don't know what I expected, but I remember falling in love with this chariot, this magical machine—and it was mine. They helped me up onto the driver's seat and then stood back shouting directions. No one told me about the mule kick, so I thought it was part of the proper mechanism and you just had to keep your left foot well out of the way. I traveled around and around that field with the kids in pursuit, yelling directions and squealing with laughter. I think I squealed a lot too, but I don't ever remember a moment of fear— only an overwhelming affection for that beautiful enchanting bucket of bolts and nuts.

"I owned it—until I went on to the next engagement—but I'll own it forever in my memory."

JUNE HAVOC *began her career as a child star in vaudeville and went on to become an actress and author.*

june havoc

"I gave up on driving. I can't do two things at one time—like talk and chew gum."

andy

"I didn't get my first car when I was sixteen, I got it when I was fifty-six. I got it last year, when I was learning to drive. Actually, I got two cars; one's a 1937 Rolls-Royce, the other's a 1970-something Rolls-Royce. They weren't expensive.

"My most memorable experience was when I was learning to drive and was out with my instructor and smashed into a taxi outside the Graybar Building in New York City. That was when I gave up on driving. I can't do two things at one time—like talk and chew gum. And I was trying to do two things at one time: drive and learn how to drive. No one was hurt, but I just got too nervous and gave up.

"So the cars are sitting up on blocks now in some garage here in town. I don't have time to go back and look at them, but I hang on to them. They're better than art."
Artist ANDY WARHOL *died in 1987 after more than fifteen minutes of fame .*

warhol

ACKNOWLEDGMENTS: Collen Cohen, Carolyn Gorry, Sue Kakstys, Elliot Kaplan, Leo Lerman, Mary Maguire, Erica Marcus, Sarah Parr, Steven Pascal, Betty A. Prashker, Rochelle Udell

PHOTO CREDITS: Dan Aykroyd (painting): Ken Danby, "From the Summer of '38," 1966, Egg Tempera Painting, 22" x 28", Private Collection; Courtesy of Gallery Moos Limited, Toronto. Doug Allen: © 1992 Doug Allen; Mario Andretti: Courtesy of Mario Andretti; Mary Kay Ash: Courtesy of Mary Kay Cosmetics; Barbie: Courtesy of Mattel Toys; James Belushi: Courtesy of the Ford Motor Company; Roy Blount Jr.: The Bettmann Archive; Erma Bombeck: Courtesy of Erma Bombeck; Dr. Joyce Brothers: The Bettmann Archive; Art Buchwald: Courtesy of the Ford Motor Company; Johnny Carson: People Weekly © 1992 Dale Wittner; Roz Chast: © 1992 Roz Chast; Richard Condon: Courtesy of Chevrolet Motor Division, General Motors Corporation; Bruce Crawford: Kirk Willis; Misha Dichter: Courtesy of Chevrolet Motor Division, General Motors Corporation; Morgan Freeman: Photofest; Debbie Gibson: Courtesy of the Ford Motor Company; John Glenn: Courtesy of John Glenn; Whoopi Goldberg: Star File/Vinnie Zufante; Andy Granatelli: Courtesy of the Free Library of Philadelphia, Automobile Reference Collection; Spalding Gray: © 1993 Paula Court; Wayne Gretsky: Courtesy of Wayne Gretsky; June Havoc: Courtesy of June Havoc; Hugh Hefner: Courtesy of Hugh Hefner; Pee-wee Herman: Janette Beckman/Outline Press; Lena Horne: Andrew Morland; Lee Iacocca: Courtesy of the Ford Motor Company; Jeremy Irons: Courtesy of the Free Library of Philadelphia, Automobile Reference Collection; Al Jarreau: Courtesy of Benno Friedman; Bela Kalman: Courtesy of Bela Kalman; Stephen King: Courtesy of Stephen King; Martin Landau: Courtesy of the Bettmann Archive; Angela Lansbury: Courtesy of Angela Lansbury; Liberace: Courtesy of the Liberace Foundation of the Performing Arts; Kelly Lynch: Deborah Feingold/Outline; Ann Magnuson: © 1993 by Brad Dunning; Branford Marsalis: Drawing by David Cowles, originally in *The New Yorker*, © 1989; John McEnroe: Courtesy of John McEnroe; Liliane Montevecchi: UPI/Bettmann News Photos; Shirley Muldowney: Richard J. Patrick; Ralph Nader: Courtesy of the New York Public Library; Gunnar Nelson: Courtesy of Chevrolet Motor Division, General Motors Corporation; Matthew Nelson: © 1991 Mark Weiss MWA; Michael O'Donoghue: Courtesy of Michael O'Donoghue; Dan Rather: Courtesy of the New York Public Library; Ronald Reagan: courtesy of the Free Library of Philadelphia, Automobile Reference Collection; Joan Rivers: © 1992 Robert Risko; Paul Rodriguez: Courtesy of Paul Rodriguez; Kenny Scharf: Courtesy of Kenny Scharf; Fisher Stevens: Courtesy of Fisher Stevens; Jackie Stewart: Focus on Sports; Jerry Stiller: Courtesy of the New York Public Library; Mark Strand: Courtesy of the New York Public Library; Lily Tomlin: © 1992 Robert Risko; Mel Torme: The Bettmann Archive; Ivana Trump: © 1990 Patrick Demarchelier, courtesy of the Free Library of Philadelphia, Automobile Reference Collection; Tommy Tune: Drawing by Eric Palma, originally in *The New Yorker*, © 1989; Vanessa Williams: Starfile/Vinnie Zufante, Courtesy of the Free Library of Philadelphia, Automobile Reference Collection; Tom Wolfe: ©1984 Charles Saxon; Andy Warhol: © 1977 Christopher Makos.